CHILDREN IN CRISIS

Living with

AIDS

Mary's Story

Helen Howard

WORLD ALMANAC® LIBRARY

Please visit our web site at: www.worldalmanaclibrary.com
For a free color catalog describing World Almanac® Library's list of high-quality books and multimedia programs, call 1-800-848-2928 (USA) or 1-800-387-3178 (Canada). World Almanac® Library's fax: (414) 332-3567.

Library of Congress Cataloging-in-Publication Data

Howard, Helen.
    Living with AIDS: Mary's story / by Helen Howard.
      p. cm. — (Children in crisis)
    Includes bibliographical references and index.
    ISBN 0-8368-5962-6 (lib. bdg.)
    1. Children of AIDS patients—South Africa—Juvenile literature. 2. AIDS (Disease)—
South Africa—Juvenile literature. I. Title. II. Children in crisis (Milwaukee, Wis.)
    RA643.86.S6H69   2005
    362.196'9792'00968—dc22   2005046330

This North American edition first published in 2006 by
World Almanac® Library
A Member of the WRC Media Family of Companies
330 West Olive Street, Suite 100
Milwaukee, WI 53212 USA

This U.S. edition copyright © 2006 by World Almanac® Library. Original edition copyright © 2005 by ticktock Entertainment Ltd. First published in 2005 by ticktock Media Ltd, Unit 2, Orchard Business Centre, North Farm Road, Tunbridge Wells, Kent TN2 3XF, U.K.

World Almanac® Library managing editor: Valerie J. Weber
World Almanac® Library art direction: Tammy West
World Almanac® Library cover design and layout: Dave Kowalski
World Almanac® Library production: Jessica Morris

Photo credits: (t=top; b=bottom; l=left; r=right): Alamy 11b, 13b, 19t, 43t; Corbis 9t, 23t, 27b, 31b, 35b, 40t, 42, 44b, 44t; Creatas 21t; Exile Images 5, 29t, 29b, 35t; Grant Law; 1, 3, 8, 9b, 10, 12, 13t, 14, 16, 18, 20, 22, 24, 26, 28, 30, 31t, 32, 34, 36, 37t, 38; The Topsy Foundation 39; United Nations Press Office 43bl; World Image Library 4, 6, 7, 11t, 15t, 15b, 17, 19b, 21b, 23b, 25t, 25b, 27t, 33t, 33b, 37b, 40b, 41t, 41b, 43b, 45.

Printed in the United States of America

1 2 3 4 5 6 7 8 9 09 08 07 06 05

The Interviewer

Elizabeth Moshe, a South African social worker employed by The Topsy Foundation, conducted the interviews with Mary, the subject of this book. A nonprofit organization, the Topsy foundation provides care for people with HIV and AIDS in the Mpumalunga Province of South Africa. Elizabeth also manages the Orphan Care Development project of Topsy's Community Outreach program.

How Mary Was Chosen for This Book

Elizabeth says: *"I interviewed Mary★ shortly after her mother's death, and I realized that she was quite depressed. At the same time, however, there was something that really impressed me about Mary—the determination to live a better life. She boldly mentioned the course [studies] she would do and all her dreams for the future."*

The Interview Process

Elizabeth says: *"The interview was a very emotional process for both Mary and me. Even though I have had quite a lot of experience with these children, it is still easy to get emotional when I have to discuss the core issues with them. The core issues are things like: 'Did your parents prepare you for their death?' or 'Is life very different now, since your parents died?' I know for a fact that it is different. Despite being very touched by the things that children like Mary tell me, it is important that I maintain my objectivity."*

★ *In order to protect her identity and as she has requested, Mary's real name has not been used in this book.*

CONTENTS

Introduction

When AIDS was first diagnosed in the 1980s, nobody could have guessed how quickly the disease would spread, infecting people all over the world. Today, most people understand that AIDS is caused by HIV, and that it can devastate families, communities, and even whole continents.

THE GLOBAL SITUATION

AIDS has already claimed more than 20 million lives worldwide; it is now the leading cause of death around the world among those ages fifteen to fify-nine. The United Nations (UN) estimates that more than 40 million men, women, and children all over the world are HIV positive, with fourteen thousand people becoming infected with the virus every day.

Currently, there is no cure for AIDS, although medical advances in treating HIV occur all the time. There is no doubt that AIDS is a global health emergency that threatens the future of the entire world.

WHAT ARE AIDS AND HIV?

AIDS stands for Acquired Immune Deficiency Syndrome and is caused by a virus called HIV, or the Human Immunodeficiency Virus. This virus damages the immune system (the part of the body that fights bacteria and infections). Many people are HIV positive but do not become ill for many years. As the HIV infection develops, the body's immune system becomes weaker and weaker until it cannot protect the body from infection anymore. Then AIDS sets in. When a person has AIDS, they are vulnerable to viruses, parasites, fungi, and bacteria that usually do not cause health problems. For a person with AIDS, these normally harmless illnesses can make a person very sick; they will eventually die.

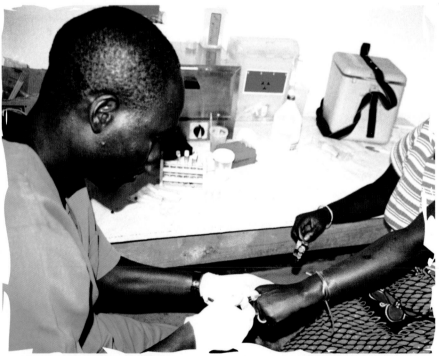

The only way to determine whether a person is HIV positive (infected with HIV) is through testing their blood for the virus.

Adults and Children Estimated to Be Living with HIV/AIDS*

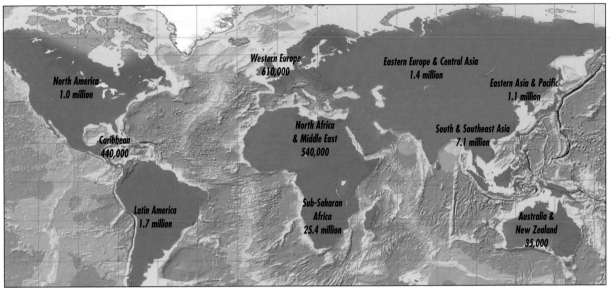

North America
1.0 million

Western Europe
610,000

Eastern Europe & Central Asia
1.4 million

Eastern Asia & Pacific
1.1 million

Caribbean
440,000

North Africa
& Middle East
540,000

South & Southeast Asia
7.1 million

Latin America
1.7 million

Sub-Saharan
Africa
25.4 million

Australia &
New Zealand
35,000

* Figures from the Joint United Nations Programme on HIV/AIDS (UNAIDS), 2004

WORST-HIT AREAS

While HIV/AIDS cases have been reported in all parts of the world, 95 percent of people living with HIV or AIDS live in low-and middle-income countries. More new HIV infections and AIDS-related deaths occur here than anywhere else.

South African schools are required by law to teach students about HIV and AIDS from the primary school level onward.

Sub-Saharan Africa is the worst-hit region in the world—home to almost 70 percent of reported cases. Epidemics are also developing in parts of Eastern Europe, such as Russia and Ukraine, and countries in Asia, such as India and Cambodia. With about 1 million infected people, North America is one of the most affected areas of the developed world.

THE ORIGINS OF AIDS

No one knows for sure how, where, or when HIV and AIDS first originated. Scientists guess that it started in either African monkeys or chimpanzees. The virus was first transmitted to humans around 1930 when someone either ate the infected animal's meat or was bitten by the animal.

The first documented case of AIDS is believed to have been in the Democratic Republic of Congo in Africa in 1959. By 1978, people in other countries were showing signs of the disease. In June 1981, doctors diagnosed HIV for the first time—in five homosexual men from the United States.

More than 12 million African children have been orphaned due to AIDS.

names, and some have even been absorbed into another country. All of this has left Africa extremely poor. The income of most Africans is four hundred to seven hundred U.S. dollars a year, making it nearly impossible for an African with AIDS to afford treatment.

AIDS education and awareness is not a priority in many parts of Africa. While the AIDS epidemic has infected millions of people throughout the continent, the greater priority for many parts of Africa is the millions of people suffering from famine.

A BRIEF HISTORY OF SOUTH AFRICA

The Republic of South Africa is located at the southern tip of the African continent. South Africa is often called the "Rainbow

THE AIDS EPIDEMIC IN AFRICA

Sub-Saharan Africa is the part of the world most affected by HIV/AIDS. Every day across the region, there are six thousand AIDS-related deaths and one thousand more people are infected with HIV. AIDS has also left millions of African children orphaned, many of whom have HIV or AIDS themselves after being infected at birth by their mother if she was HIV positive.

National HIV rates vary greatly between African countries. In Somalia and the Gambia, 2 percent of the adult population is infected. In South Africa and Zambia, about 20 percent of the adult population is infected. African countries with the highest infection rates include Swaziland (39 percent), Botswana (37 percent), Lesotho (29 percent), and Zimbabwe (25 percent).

REASONS FOR AFRICA'S AIDS EPIDEMIC

Civil war has plagued many parts of Africa for years. Countries have changed boundaries and

SOUTH AFRICA: FACTS AND FIGURES

Population:	**41 million**
Capital city:	**Pretoria**
Ethnicities:	**75 percent black, 13 percent white, 8 percent mixed race, 3 percent Indian**
Official languages:	**Afrikaans, English, Ndebele, North Sotho, South Sotho, Swazi, Tsonga, Venda, Xhosa, and Zulu**
Religions:	**Christianity, Islam, Hinduism, Judaism and traditional religions**
Climate:	**Temperate**
Geography:	**Vast plains rimmed by rugged hills and narrow coastal plain**

In the poorest parts of Africa, millions of people are starving to death.

Nation" because of its wide mix of cultures. This ethnic diversity has also caused hundreds of years of war, however.

When Dutch settlers arrived in the mid-seventeenth century, South Africa was inhabited by many indigenous tribes, including the Khoi, San, Xhosa, and Zulu peoples. The Dutch immediately asserted their authority over the native tribes.

The discovery of diamonds and gold in the region encouraged mass immigration and intensified the oppression of native peoples. This discrimination against native South Africans came to be called apartheid; a legal system that kept races separate and meant that black and *coloured* (a South African term for mixed-race) people had fewer rights than white people.

The 1990s brought an end to apartheid. South Africa became a democracy where, according to law, all races had the same rights. In 1994, Nelson Mandela became South Africa's first democratically elected president.

AIDS TIME LINE

1981 A mysterious disorder affecting the immune system claims the lives of five men in the United States.

1982 Scientists name the new illness "AIDS" (Acquired Immune Deficiency Syndrome). They find that AIDS can be transmitted through sexual intercourse or by infected blood.

1983 It is discovered that HIV causes AIDS.

1985 The United States begins testing blood samples for HIV.

1988 World AIDS Day is introduced to focus attention on fighting the disease.

1991 Ten million people worldwide are HIV positive.

2000 More than 21.8 million people have died of AIDS since the late 1970s; infection rates increase in Eastern Europe, Russia, India, and Southeast Asia.

2001 Drug companies begin to offer discounted AIDS drugs to developing countries. During the year, 3 million people die from AIDS, including 2.3 million in sub-Saharan Africa.

2002 It is reported that almost half of all HIV-infected adults are now female.

2003 Swaziland has the world's highest rate of HIV—almost four out of ten adults are infected.

2004 South Africa provides free antiretrovirals in hospitals. (Antiretrovirals are the drugs used to treat people with HIV). UNAIDS (Joint United Nations Programme on HIV/AIDS) reports that 25 million people have died from AIDS since 1981 and that 38 million are HIV positive.

CHAPTER ONE: **Meet Mary**

In Africa, more than 25 million people have died of AIDS since it was first discovered. More than 12 million children have lost one or both parents to the disease. Mary became one of these statistics when her mother died of AIDS only six months before this interview took place. While not technically an orphan, Mary has never really known her father, who lives far away. Today, Mary lives with her maternal grandmother and cousins, who also lost their parents to AIDS.

Mary does a lot of the cooking and housework in the house she shares with her grandmother and cousins.

MARY SAYS:

"My name is Mary and I am fourteen years old. I was born at Philadelphia Hospital in the town of Dennilton in the province of Mpumalanga, South Africa. I grew up in Balfour, also in Mpumalanga. I am a good-hearted person and love people. I believe that out of love comes respect.

Others would probably describe me as a respectful and caring child. I can speak Zulu, Ndebele, and English. I like singing, playing with other children, watching television, and writing poetry. I like music, particularly gospel and R&B. I also enjoy sports, especially soccer. I play soccer for the girls' team at school."

EXTENDED FAMILIES

In South Africa, the average age at which someone dies of AIDS is thirty-seven, which means that a generation of children is left without parents to bring them up. In most cases, extended families step in at these times, fulfilling a duty that is a part of most African cultures.

Typically, a grandmother takes in her orphaned grandchildren after her daughter dies. As today's grandparents die of old age, however, these children are often left once more without a guardian.

When children are orphaned by AIDS, aunts, uncles, and grandparents often step in to raise them as their own.

When orphans have no extended family to turn to, it often falls to older children to raise their younger siblings.

GROWING UP TOO SOON

When their parents die, some AIDS orphans do not have an extended family that is able or willing to take care of them. Child-headed households are becoming more common in areas with high numbers of AIDS deaths.

Even if governments had the funds to build more orphanages, there is no evidence that this would be an ideal solution for orphaned children. Many argue that the best way to ensure that recently bereaved children are not too emotionally scarred is to help them to carry on in some form of family life.

"My mother passed away on July 31 , 2004. My father is still alive but doesn't stay with us any more. He lives far away in KwaNdebele. He stayed with my mother from the time she was twenty-two until she was twenty-five years old, when my mother gave birth to me. I don't have any full brothers and sisters. I only have a half-brother called Lucky.

I live with my granny, my mother's mother. We live in a normal home. My cousins Nhlanhla (twenty-five), Lindiwe (eighteen), and Buti (fourteen) also live with us. I am very close to my cousins, and we enjoy each other's company. We have quite a strong, healthy bond, and we can talk freely about anything that is on our minds. We live in an RDP home [low-cost government house], which also has a shack attached to it; this is where my granny sleeps. I sleep in the house, in the same bed as Lindiwe. We have a TV and radio at home, although the TV is not working at the moment.

In 1996, I visited my father and his family in KwaNdebele, which is about 400 kilometers [250 miles] away from Siyathemba, which is where we live. Some cultural rituals were performed for me when I went to KwaNdebele.

Afterward, I returned to live with my grandmother. In 1998, I again went to visit my father, but when I got there he disappeared, and no one knew where he was. I haven't been back since."

Mary and her family live in a Reconstruction and Development Programme (RDP) house. These basic tin and brick houses were part of a postapartheid program to improve housing in South Africa's poor townships.

TESTING FOR HIV

HIV is usually detected through a blood test, administered by a medical professional. If HIV antibodies are detected in the blood, the person is HIV positive. If the first test is positive, a second test is usually performed to make sure that there were no mistakes the first time.

The South African government has introduced certain laws to support testing for HIV, but testing is not compulsory. The law requires that whenever people are tested, they receive counseling and that their tests and results are completely confidential. It is illegal in South Africa to test someone for HIV without their consent. Similarly, a child cannot be tested without the written consent of his or her parent.

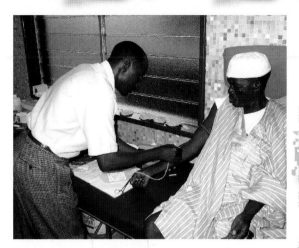

To test a person for HIV, a doctor or nurse extracts blood from a patient's veins and then has it tested for the virus in a laboratory.

Antiretroviral drugs are the only effective way of extending and improving the quality of life for those infected with HIV.

ANTIRETROVIRAL DRUGS

The only medicines for treating HIV are antiretroviral drugs. These drugs act by slowing down the development of the virus within the body. There are currently about fourteen different types of these drugs.

During much of the 1990s, most people with HIV, especially patients in developing countries, could not afford antiretroviral drugs. Recently, many governments and aid organizations have made agreements with drug companies to make the medicines available to developing countries at much lower prices than usual. In 2003, President Thabo Mbeki of South Africa authorized giving antiretroviral drugs for free to all HIV-positive people. As of 2005, this decision had not been put into practice.

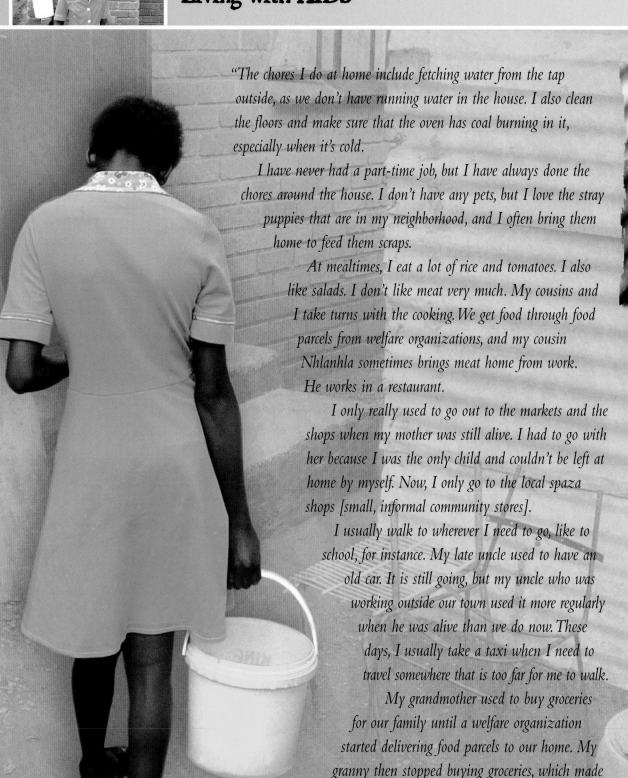

"The chores I do at home include fetching water from the tap outside, as we don't have running water in the house. I also clean the floors and make sure that the oven has coal burning in it, especially when it's cold.

I have never had a part-time job, but I have always done the chores around the house. I don't have any pets, but I love the stray puppies that are in my neighborhood, and I often bring them home to feed them scraps.

At mealtimes, I eat a lot of rice and tomatoes. I also like salads. I don't like meat very much. My cousins and I take turns with the cooking. We get food through food parcels from welfare organizations, and my cousin Nhlanhla sometimes brings meat home from work. He works in a restaurant.

I only really used to go out to the markets and the shops when my mother was still alive. I had to go with her because I was the only child and couldn't be left at home by myself. Now, I only go to the local spaza shops [small, informal community stores].

I usually walk to wherever I need to go, like to school, for instance. My late uncle used to have an old car. It is still going, but my uncle who was working outside our town used it more regularly when he was alive than we do now. These days, I usually take a taxi when I need to travel somewhere that is too far for me to walk.

My grandmother used to buy groceries for our family until a welfare organization started delivering food parcels to our home. My granny then stopped buying groceries, which made me angry because now we don't have enough food.

Mary is very diligent about carrying out her household chores.

Although she doesn't have any pets of her own, Mary likes playing with some of the stray dogs in the neighborhood.

"If I am sad or angry, I will withdraw from people's company. I go to a quiet place and sit by myself where I can think. When an adult shouts at me or reprimands me for something, it makes me sad. I also feel sad when children of my age talk about their mothers, as I lost mine. I also get upset when my grandmother talks about my mother being a rebellious child who didn't abide by her rules.

The last time I cried was in November. It was a Monday and some people were asking questions about my past. They specifically asked me about my mother, and I cried."

FACTS: AN INSTANT DEATH SENTENCE?

When AIDS was first identified, people believed that contracting HIV meant an instant death sentence. Today, much more can be done to delay the onset of AIDS and prolong the life of the patient.

• It is possible to be HIV positive but not know it for many years. Warning signs include sudden unexplained loss of weight, a dry cough, recurring fever or night sweats, and extreme and constant tiredness. The only way to know for certain is to have an HIV test.

• Most people with HIV who are diagnosed early and receive proper treatment live more than sixteen years from the day of their infection. Many will live an average lifespan.

• In developed countries, 50 percent of people with HIV who do not receive treatment will develop AIDS in ten years and 70 percent in fourteen years. Once their AIDS has developed, 94 percent of all patients die within five years. This rate of progression is generally much faster in drug users and in people from developing countries.

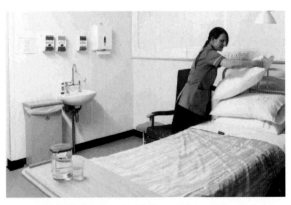

More medical facilities are available to HIV-positive people in wealthy countries than to those in developing countries.

"My father and mother were both Ndebeles, which has its own cultural norms and values. One of the things we Ndebeles do when a baby is born is to take the new baby to the graveyard, where his or her ancestors are buried. This is to show the ancestors that there is a new family member, so that they may bless the baby and offer it protection. On the same day, a sheep is slaughtered. The sheep's bile and blood is mixed together and rubbed on the baby's shaven head and then over the baby's entire body. It brings luck. Periodically, we visit the graves of our ancestors and ask blessings from them. I don't know what is done when Ndebeles get married because I am not yet married, and I haven't asked.

My people used to respect their cultural inheritance more than they do now. They also used to wear traditional clothes, which they don't often do any more. For special occasions or festivals such

Mary is proud of her cultural heritage, although she is aware that her people do not acknowledge their culture as much as they once did.

as the birth of a baby we celebrate by slaughtering a sheep. We also slaughtered a sheep recently when my cousin was involved in an accident and survived. We slaughtered the sheep to thank the ancestors for protecting him. When someone dies, we slaughter a cow and cook the meat for those who will be attending the funeral. We serve it with lots of salads and vegetable dishes, as well as traditional home-brewed beer. I believe that when a person dies, he or she joins and becomes part of our ancestors."

THE CULTURES OF SOUTH AFRICA

South Africa is a country boasting many different cultures, all evident in an amazing range of arts, crafts, dance, music, food, and sports. Three-fourths of South Africa's 49 million people are blacks whose ancestors arrived from Central Africa up to fifteen hundred years ago.

Most black South Africans fall into two major ethnic groups: the Nguni, which consist of Zulu, Xhosa, Ndebele, and Swazi peoples; and the Sotho, which includes the North Sotho, Venda, and South Sotho or Basotho peoples. Cultural ceremonies play an important role in the lives of black South Africans and are often marked by special clothing and accessories.

The many cultures of South Africa have their own traditional costumes and dances.

The Ndebele culture is known for its distinctive beadwork, used to make jewelry.

THE NDEBELE PEOPLE

The history of the Ndebele people goes back to the early 1600s. Between 1880 and 1890, there were several battles between the Ndebele and the white rulers of the then-Transvaal Republic. After they were defeated, the Ndebeles were forced to work and live on farms; this restriction destroyed their pride as a nation. It was only in 1984, when the KwaNdebele Homeland was established, that this pride was restored and the people moved back there. The Ndebele people are well known for their artistic talent, especially as displayed in their painted houses and colorful beadwork.

Living with AIDS

"The name of my school is Isifisosethu Secondary School, and it is situated about one kilometer from where I live. I normally walk to school with my cousin Lindiwe and my friend Letia. The school has about eight hundred students attending, and there are about thirty-six students in my class. I really enjoy school. I am currently in the tenth grade and my teacher's name is Mam Shabangu. My favorite subject is English. I also enjoy human and social sciences.

I believe I am a good, hard-working student and I have been a prefect since I was in the eighth grade [at primary school]. I am a born leader and was asked to be a mediator between the school governing body and my fellow students. I think I am a good example to the other kids.

I take the responsibility of being a prefect very seriously and always make sure that I look neat and tidy in my school uniform and abide by all of the school rules. I enjoy reading books, especially Cinderella and Snow White.

My friends are Thokozile, Yvonne, Elsie, Esther, Nombulelo, Busi, Sarah, and Zanele. My friends and I enjoy drama and singing. Our teachers trust us and give us a lot of responsibility. We play netball in the community playground and do drama in our school grounds and in classes.

Once we went on a school trip to the Sterkfontein Caves, where the Cradle of Humankind is located. That was a real adventure for me that I will never forget. It is the place where the very first adult apeman was found in 1936, and fossils have been found there that date back to more than three million years ago."

Mary takes her schooling very seriously and continues to get top grades in all her subjects.

The majority of classrooms in the South African townships are overcrowded, and schools are restricted by limited budgets, despite government promises to greatly improve educational standards nationwide.

SUBSTANDARD SCHOOLING

When apartheid was the system of government in South Africa, education was used as a tool to oppress black people. Millions had fewer educational opportunities than whites and were not encouraged to pursue further education. Today, more than ten years after the end of apartheid, township and rural schools still contain mainly, if not only, black and coloured students.

For decades, a shortage of teachers, classrooms, and equipment plagued poor communities. Since apartheid ended, South Africa has committed the largest single segment of its national budget to education.

By 2000, ten thousand classrooms had been built or repaired, new textbooks had been published, and new methods of training teachers had been put in place. Despite these improvements, however, there is still a long way to go toward creating equal educational opportunities for all South Africans. Today, township schools still suffer from a lack of facilities, overcrowded classrooms, and tight budgets.

South Africa has a total of 12 million students and about twenty-eight thousand schools. Children usually begin school at the age of seven and are supposed to attend until they are fifteen.

CHAPTER TWO: Being Left Behind

Pandemic is the word used to describe the spread of a disease over a whole country or large part of the world. There is no question that the world is facing an AIDS pandemic today, one that has orphaned more than 15 million children, 95 percent of whom live in Africa. The emotional trauma experienced by these young people is immense, and the huge changes introduced into their lives are difficult to accept. Orphaned children are often brought up by grandparents and aunts, but when this isn't possible, some older children have to raise their younger siblings themselves.

MARY SAYS:

"The day my mother passed away was the saddest day of my life. When I am sad, I usually talk to myself, or I take a picture of my mother and talk to it as if she is there to listen.

Presently, nothing really makes me happy. I haven't been happy for a long time. I was happy when my mother was still alive. I would be happy because my mother used to buy me gifts and take me places. Even when I heard that I had progressed very well academically this year, I remained sad. It was just another normal day for me."

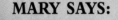

Mary suffers greatly from the loss of her mother a few months before this book was written. Luckily, she has family to whom she can turn for companionship.

A growing death rate due to AIDS has meant that many of South Africa's cemeteries are filling up much faster than expected.

BEING LITTLE

Being little is so nice.
You get all the love you need.
And all comfort you need.
But when it's time it is time.
For a minute I was the happiest child.
But my whole life, I will be the saddest.
And crying, until today I am still crying.
Love from a parent is what counts.
I did get all the love from my loving mother.
But in the middle of the road,
I lost everything I had
But I haven't lost my life.

– by Mary, 2004

FACTS: AIDS WORLDWIDE

When AIDS was first identified, very little was known about the mysterious disease. Twenty years later, much more is known, and research continues worldwide.

• AIDS is the fourth leading cause of death around the world.

• At the end of 2004, 25.4 million people were living with AIDS or HIV in sub-Saharan Africa, compared to 1 million in North America and 40 million worldwide.

• In Africa, 20 percent more women than men are living with HIV.

• The area with the fastest increase in HIV rates is in eastern Asia, especially in China, Indonesia, and Vietnam.

• Central Asia and Eastern Europe, particularly Russia and Ukraine, are also experiencing steep increases, fueled by a rising number of intravenous drug users.

• By 2007, it is estimated that it will cost 20 billion U.S. dollars to effectively fight the AIDS pandemic in developing countries.

These AIDS orphans from Cambodia live in one of the many orphanages run by churches and volunteers.

"When my mother was sick I knew that she would pass away soon because she told me so. When she was ill, all she could take were painkillers like Compral [a type of mild aspirin], so she was in a lot of pain and discomfort.

Even though I expected my mother's death, I wasn't prepared for it. I had a dream that my mother would not die until I had finished school, got a job, and saved enough money to buy her a nice house. I really didn't want her to die.

My mother had an old house and a few pieces of old furniture, and before she died she wrote her will declaring me as the one to benefit of those things, but only when I turn twenty-one.

The will hasn't been legalized; it's just written on a piece of paper. I have asked a social worker and my pastor to help me legalize it. My granny does not know about the will because my mother told me not to say anything to her until the document is legalized.

The other thing my mother did before she died was to apply for a government grant. She was supposed to have received it in September last year, but when she passed away in July 2004, she still hadn't received anything. My granny went to the government office to change the details of the payee for the grant. The grant still hasn't been paid yet, but my granny has all of the papers as proof that we did apply. My mother never left any money for me, because the last time she worked was at the beginning of 2004."

In her will, Mary's mother requested that a family member live with Mary until she is twenty-one years old.

ALTERNATIVE MEDICINES

Many believe that traditional and alternative African medicines could help treat HIV.

Some people have criticized HIV drugs as being even more damaging to the body than the virus itself. The South African health minister recently stated that the use of traditional African medicines may eventually replace antiretroviral drugs in the treatment of HIV and AIDS.

Many traditional healers in South Africa believe that the media plays down the role of natural therapies in combating AIDS. South Africa's Medical Research Council is reviewing ten natural or alternative remedies that claim to help AIDS patients. One remedy is a plant called *Sutherlandia microphylla,* which may increase energy, appetite, and body mass in people living with HIV. While many people with HIV take this plant, however, it has been known to interact badly with some antiretroviral drugs. Other natural remedies for treating AIDS include beets and lemons.

TURNING TO RELIGION

Many people dying of AIDS and their families turn to religion for comfort and meaning throughout their difficulties. This can be especially true in cultures where the stigma associated with AIDS means that people are reluctant to speak openly about it among their friends and families. Talking to children about subjects like death and sex is simply not done in many sub-Saharan cultures. Many children therefore feel isolated and confused about what happened to their parents when they died. Religion can offer explanations for what happens after death, which can be very comforting for bereaved and grieving children.

Many AIDS orphans find solace in religion, like these children pictured with their minister.

"My life has changed dramatically since my mother died. She used to do everything in her power to give me a good life, even when she had no money. Whenever she had money, she always made sure that my school fees were paid and that I had clothes to wear and food to eat.

The fact that I cannot see my mother, be her loved child, is a deep pain for me. When children my age speak about their mothers I feel like running away and hiding. I used to come home happy and expecting to see her when I got home, but now I am constantly reminded that this is not going to happen. It makes me feel so sad all the time. There is no question that my life has changed for the worse now. If I could have one wish in the world, it would be that my mother could come back.

I am a Christian and I go to church from time to time. I don't understand much about religion. I go to church because my granny says so. I believe in God because when my mother was really sick and in pain, God decided to take my mother to him, so that she may be healed and have no more pain.

There are people from the Topsy Foundation [a nonprofit organization that works to help victims of HIV and their families] who visit me regularly to make sure I am okay. These people are Elizabeth Moshe and Pinkie, who is a field worker with Topsy. It is always helpful. Recently, Topsy bought my school uniform for me. My granny is sometimes moody. It sometimes happens that if a social worker comes for a visit or takes me somewhere, when I come back, I'll find my granny in a happy mood. Some people don't want Western organizations to help our community, but I think they are just jealous of those who get help.

I don't know how many other children are orphans because they have lost their parents to AIDS. As far as I have experienced, orphaned children are not treated differently in my community."

Mary is a Christian and believes that her mother has gone to heaven, where she no longer suffers pain.

Teaching children about AIDS is one way to try to prevent further spread of the HIV virus.

AIDS EDUCATION

There are many AIDS-awareness campaigns run by government and aid organizations. For example, the South Africa Health Education Programme is a community-based project that uses games and activities to present the issues associated with AIDS and HIV to young people in a sensitive way. While increasing numbers of young people are now educated about HIV/AIDS, the true challenge is to make sure they put their knowledge into practice in real life. Life-skills education, which incorporates HIV/AIDS education, is now a compulsory part of the South African school curriculum taught at primary and secondary schools.

AIDS PREVENTION

One government program in Uganda is the "ABC" campaign, which stands for "Abstinence, Be faithful, or use Condoms." This program has spread to many other parts of the world.

A condom is a sheath worn during sex to prevent the exchange of body fluids.Using condoms usually prevents HIV from being transmitted. One disadvantage of the male condom is the fact that only men can really control its use. An alternative is the female condom, but it is ten times more expensive than the male one. Although condoms are the single most effective defense against HIV, many countries impose restrictions on their distribution.

The "ABC" campaign has been very successful in educating young people about HIV and AIDS, although it has also been widely criticized.

CHAPTER THREE: AIDS in the Community

AIDS has always had a stigma attached, due to the fact that HIV is most commonly contracted through sexual intercourse. Many cultures maintain that certain subjects, such as sex, should not be discussed publicly and not with children. This culture of silence can mean that some HIV/AIDS victims suffer their burden alone because they fear they will be shunned by their family or community. It is only through education, understanding, and public recognition of the issue that the rapidly spreading virus might possibly be curbed.

MARY SAYS:

"I only know one person who has died of AIDS, although I suspect that a second person I know also died because of it. I have never seen any problems that arise because a person died of AIDS in my community. I suppose the only real problem is the fact that many people are afraid to talk about it. I don't know why this is the case.

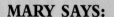
Mary cannot understand why many of the older people in her community are afraid to talk about AIDS and HIV publicly.

When people are sick or dying of AIDS, they usually require full-time care. Many social service agencies and religious organizations offer in-home nursing and caregiving services.

The sick people in our community go to the clinic for treatment or to the hospital. When a person is sick, the family take care of the person.

Sometimes home-based care workers help with the general care of the person. It is painful when there is a sick person in the home, especially when the thought of 'this person is going to die' comes. But I believe if one of the family members is sick, we must love, care for and feed them. We must also give them everything they ask for, as this will help them emotionally."

FACTS: WOMEN AND AIDS

Early in the epidemic, men vastly outnumbered women among people infected with HIV. Today, nearly 50 percent of adults living with HIV globally are women; that number reaches nearly 60 percent in sub-Saharan Africa. There are a number of reasons:

• Women are more likely to get HIV from men than men are from women.

• Women and girls all over the world, but particularly in developing countries, are at risk of being forced to have sex against their will, exposing them to the virus through infected men. South Africa is reported to have one of the highest number of rape cases in the world.

• Sometimes women and girls are so desperate for food, money, housing, or other things essential for survival that they offer to have sex with someone in exchange for these necessities.

• In cultures where women have fewer rights than men, they can feel powerless to ensure that men use condoms during sexual intercourse to prevent transmission of HIV.

If a woman is pregnant when she is infected with HIV, there is a high chance the baby will be HIV positive, too.

Living with AIDS

"When neighbors and people from the community come to visit a person who is dying, they tend to offer all kinds of encouragement. It is easy for the family and the person who is ill to become uplifted and reassured by this. People often say, 'This person will be fine' because that is what everyone wants to believe. This also makes you believe they will not die.

The home-based care workers are the first people that come to help take care of sick people in our community. The local doctors are our second level of care. We do get indirect help from overseas, in the form of financial aid. The home-based care workers are all local African people.

I know AIDS kills. It leaves children orphaned. I know that HIV is transmitted via the blood. Therefore, if an HIV-negative person gets a blood transfusion using HIV-contaminated blood, then they will contract HIV. By practicing safe sex and by abstaining from sex, people can protect themselves from catching HIV.

I think someone will discover a cure for AIDS one day. But I also think that when we find that cure, there will be another incurable disease that will come about.

Some people believe that sharing utensils with a person who has AIDS will give them AIDS. Some also believe that if you eat food that has been left by an HIV-positive person, you will contract AIDS. Other wrong beliefs include sharing the same bed, or hugging someone."

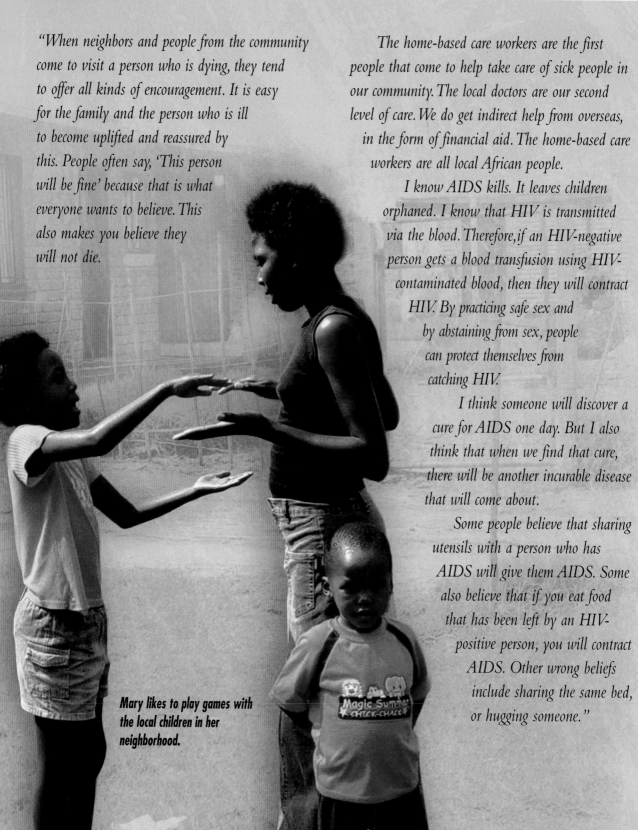

Mary likes to play games with the local children in her neighborhood.

THE SHAME OF IT

From the moment that AIDS was first identified, there has been a stigma associated with the disease. It is important that this stigma is erased because secrecy and shame often prevent people from finding out their HIV status. Many people refuse to be tested because they fear that if they are HIV positive, they will embarass themselves and their families. Fear and shame can also compel some people to completely avoid family members and friends with AIDS or HIV.

Because AIDS has always been associated with sex, and especially because it was originally associated with male homosexuality, it is even a greater taboo subject for many cultures. The truth is that anyone can contract HIV—it does not discriminate in terms of gender, race, country, or sexuality.

Because of the shame traditionally associated with HIV and AIDS, many people are currently living without knowing that they are HIV positive.

Nelson Mandela wants to break the culture of silence that surrounds the AIDS pandemic.

BREAKING THE SILENCE

When Nelson Mandela's son died of AIDS in early 2005, Mandela publicly challenged the widespread taboo in South Africa and Africa that keeps many Africans from discussing the disease and the epidemic. The political activist and former president of South Africa said that until people start regarding AIDS like any other disease, such as tuberculosis or cancer, and stop trying to hide it out of shame, more people will continue to suffer in silence. The rapidly increasing problem will only get worse. A poor understanding of the disease, prejudice, sensationalist media reporting, and fears relating to AIDS-related illness and death also fuel people's anxieties about AIDS.

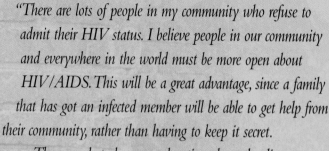

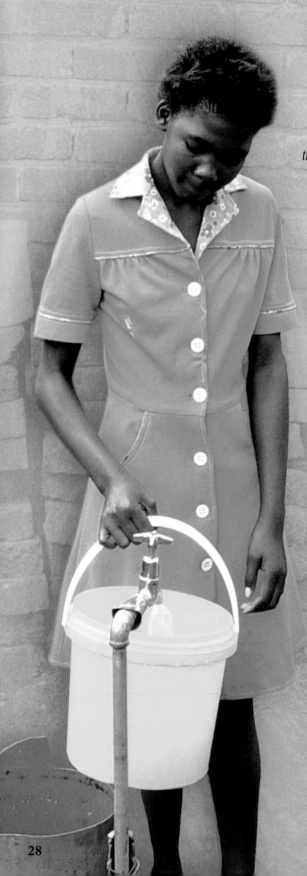

"There are lots of people in my community who refuse to admit their HIV status. I believe people in our community and everywhere in the world must be more open about HIV/AIDS. This will be a great advantage, since a family that has got an infected member will be able to get help from their community, rather than having to keep it secret.

There needs to be more education about the disease. I think people will be more open if they are informed. I learned about AIDS and HIV last year at school from my teachers.

In my community, men and women don't have equal rights. Men in my community always complain and say children have rights equal to theirs, and they hate that because they feel that they are the heads of households and must be the rulers. Men still beat their children like animals, and if children tell their fathers that they will report it to the police, they tell the children to go and ask the government to be their parents. Children are not allowed to talk back to an adult or they are reprimanded. In fact, a child must never talk to an adult like they would talk to a peer. Approach and vocabulary must be different between the two."

Mary's family has no running water at home, so they must take buckets to a nearby faucet.

HIV AND SEX

The most common method of getting HIV is through having sex without a condom with an infected partner. Prostitutes (or sex workers) are particularly vulnerable to catching and passing on the virus.

Prostitution is illegal in most countries, including South Africa. Sex workers thus have few legal and social rights and are often forced to operate in secret.

Many people believe some dangerous myths about how AIDS can be cured. One of these beliefs is that having sex with a virgin, a girl or young woman who has never had sex, can cure someone infected with HIV. This belief has provoked many acts of rape against young women and girls. If the rapist is HIV positive, there is a high chance that the rape victim will become infected with the virus, too.

This woman was infected with HIV after being raped. She is now a counselor who works with survivors of rape.

HIV AND DRUGS

Another way that HIV can be contracted is through sharing an intravenous needle (used to inject drugs such as heroin or cocaine) with someone who is HIV positive. Intravenous drug use is not as high in South Africa as it is in many parts of Asia and the United States because many of the commonly injected drugs were unavailable in South Africa under apartheid.

In many parts of the world, needle-exchange programs have been introduced to encourage drug users to go to special centers to swap their used needles for clean ones. Evidence suggests that these programs have been successful. They have caused some controversy because some people fear they encourage drug use.

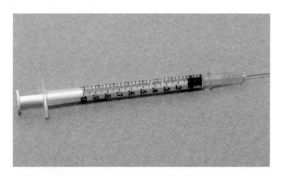

One way HIV can be passed on is when intravenous drug users who have the virus share their needles with someone else.

CHAPTER FOUR: No Place Like Home

Growing up in a South African township where the number of AIDS and HIV cases is extremely high inevitably takes its toll on the local people. Apartheid, the set of laws introduced to South Africa in 1948, meant that many basic rights—like health care and education—were denied or limited for black and coloured South Africans. Although apartheid was dismantled in 1994, the number of AIDS cases in poverty-stricken townships continues to rise.

MARY SAYS:

"I live in Siyathemba, which means 'We have hope.' Siyathemba has a population of approximately five thousand people.

The closest big city to our township is Johannesburg. I have only ever passed through Johannesburg on the way to other smaller cities.

Mary often stops to look at the items on sale at her local store on her way home from school.

The township of Siyathemba where Mary lives is very poor and run-down.

Johannesburg is a glamorous place where all of the soap opera stars live.

Siyathemba has some basic resources like a clinic, schools, a church, and playgrounds, but they are all in bad condition. Most people live in shacks or matchbox-sized houses. I wish there were hotels and a good, big hospital and an airport.

There is nothing good about Siyathemba. It is a dirty, untidy place. There are few places that are clean. It is also uncivilized.

In order to improve life in my community, there would need to be more job opportunities, and our people would need to learn how to respect one another more—only then would it be a better life."

FACTS: AFTER APARTHEID

The end of apartheid in South Africa in 1994, was supposed to mean the beginning of equality for all races. In many ways, however, a better life has been slow in coming to many poor communities:

• The average black household has become 15 percent poorer since 1994, while the average white household has become wealthier by 19 percent. South Africa is still a country of "two nations" divided along racial lines.

• Millions of black and coloured people still live in shacks with no access to water or proper sanitation.

• Today, while 6.2 percent of the white population is infected with HIV/AIDS, more than 12.9 percent of the black population is HIV positive.

• There has always been a high level of crime in South Africa, but since the end of apartheid, it has been increasing. Nearly twenty-two thousand murders occur there every year, more than in the United States, which has nearly seven times more people.

Under apartheid, signs designated where different races were allowed to go.

"Among my people, there are many cultural values, which need to be respected. For instance, men are not allowed to enter anybody's house wearing a hat, not even in their own home. Only women are allowed to cover their heads inside the house. Usually, a grandfather has his own separate seat made from an old tree trunk. A girl is not allowed to sit on this chair, which is called a gciki.

In terms of how things have changed since apartheid, all I can say is that change is not easy. The beginning of this year we had new white teachers at our school. The reason I indicate that they were new is because there is another white teacher who's been working there for some time [the vice principal]. The children wanted to go on strike because they did not like the new white teachers. The vice principal warned the group that if they did strike, they would be suspended or even removed from the school register. So, I believe in some places racism still has traces.

Another incidence of racism concerns a girl who lives in the same street as me. She is about sixteen years old. One day last year, she was sent to Balfour [a largely white town near Siyathemba]. She says she was walking down the street when a white girl slapped her on the face so hard for no apparent reason."

Mary walks to school every day with her friends. She enjoys school and is well respected by her teachers and her peers.

HISTORY OF THE TOWNSHIPS

South African townships developed as a result of racial oppression. In1948, a new law forced different races to live and operate separately, in the beginning of what is called apartheid or what black South Africans often refer to as "The Struggle."

Although the 1952 Group Areas Act (which forced blacks into the townships) has now been abolished, most communities still remain segregated. A large proportion of the black and coloured population remains poor. Ten years of democracy and racial freedom has slowly begun to change this division, but it will take the government's time and perseverance to further improve this unequal situation.

In 1952, many people protested against the Group Areas Act, which forced housing and education to be separated according to race.

A HARD LIFE

Hundreds of thousands of black South Africans live in overcrowded townships, which are shantytowns on the outskirts of major cities. Poverty here is often high, housing is of a low standard, and many live without running water or electricity. Unemployment and crime levels are also high. Progress is being made to improve the quality of life for these communities. Considering that it is more than sixty years since apartheid forced black South Africans to live in these townships, progress has been slow.

Unfortunately, in communities where poverty is rife and HIV education is lacking, disease and illnesses spread quickly. HIV infection rates in South Africa's townships are among the highest in the world.

Life is tough in South African townships or shanty towns. Few houses have running water or electricity. Sewage systems are poor or nonextistent

Living with AIDS

"I miss my mother very much. At my grandmother's house, things are done differently from my mother's house, and that makes me miss home.

Before Topsy came to our community, there were people who really struggled and were not getting help, especially sick people.

I do not think our people are proud of their culture. This is because I have never heard or seen any cultural celebrations or anything similar in my community. I think our people are somewhere between Western and African cultures.

My grandmother was reluctant to help my mother when she was sick. Sometimes when my mother asked for money to pay the electricity bill, my grandmother would refuse. When she heard that Topsy was giving us food parcels when they found out that my mother was sick, she started showing care and was loving toward my mother. She had never done this before.

I never really worry about getting sick. But when I think about death, it makes me scared. I feel like running away."

Mary is a role model to many of the younger children in her community.

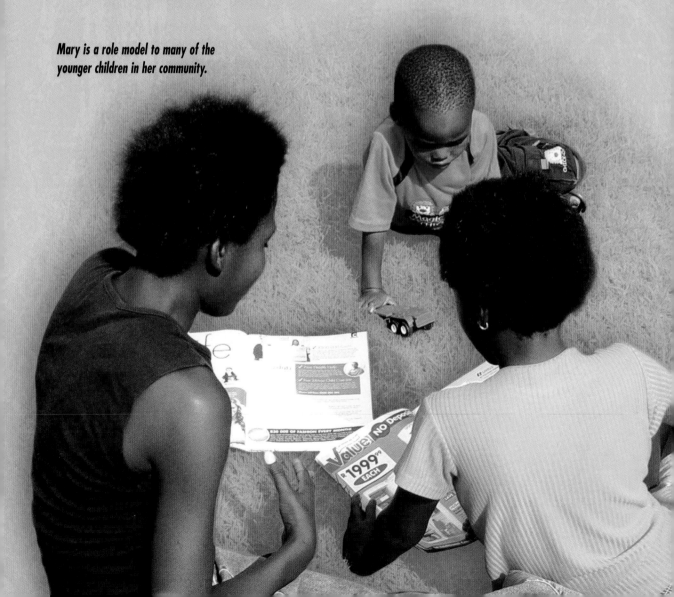

LOSS AND CHANGE

Children who lose one or both parents to AIDS are affected in many ways. The most obvious shift for them is the change in their living situation. Grandparents or other family members raise these children, or the youngsters continue life without an adult at home.

Their trauma usually starts a long time before a parent dies. During their parent's illness, children are often forced to sell assets for medicine and assume household and child-care responsibilities beyond their years. Through all these difficulties, there is often not a lot of time or consideration given to the psychological impact on the child. People in many African cultures belive that they should not talk to children about death. Sometimes, young children are not included in discussions about the imminent or recent death of their parent.

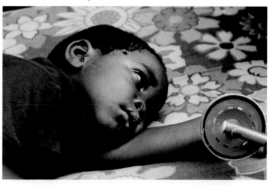

Many African cultures believe that children should be protected from the facts surrounding their parent's illness.

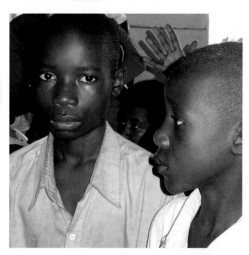

Many young people suffer great emotional trauma and feel they have no one to turn to when they are orphaned by AIDS.

THE EFFECT ON SOCIETY

The wider effects on society of the growing number of "AIDS orphans" are difficult to pin down. A huge proportion of a generation is growing up without parents, however, suggesting a big impact on cultures around the world.

Considerable evidence shows that many extended families are unable to cope with caring for orphaned children. These children then suffer the instability of being moved from family member to family member, giving them a sense of not belonging or being loved anymore. Many people fear this psychological trauma will result in a massive increase in the number of children beoming delinquent, dropping out of school, or even becoming criminals.

"My daily routine usually goes along these lines: I wake up, do some light chores like sweeping the floors, then I cook something for breakfast. While the food is cooking, I have a bath and put my school uniform on. I then eat my breakfast and leave for school. During the school vacations, I wake up and clean my room and my granny's room. I also do chores like cooking. Afterward, I rest. As the day passes, I visit friends during the day, then I come home to rest and sleep.

I do not usually keep up with world news. The television at home is currently broken, and I am not keen on listening to the radio. I occasionally read the newspapers, for instance, I really like the jokes that are often in there. There is a comic strip called 'Crux' in the Daily Sun newspaper and I always enjoy it. My favorite joke is about a gentleman sitting in his car reading a newspaper when an armed gunman approaches him and says, 'Hijack!' The man then replies, 'Hi! But my name isn't Jack, it's John.'

I used to play soccer for the ladies' club, but the teacher who used to coach us is no longer willing to. As part of community activities, I take part in an art and drama group, which sometimes takes place after school.

Mary finds it easy to make friends, although when she is sad, she prefers to be by herself instead of talking about how she is feeling.

Mary enjoys many extracurricular activities, such as sports, art, and drama, but she feels happiest when she is at school.

I imagine what my life as an adult would be like all the time. When I grow up, I would like to be a mechanical engineer, and I truly believe that I have the talent, dedication, and intelligence to become one.

I haven't yet decided where I would like to live when I am old enough to make those kinds of decisions. However, I do know that I don't ever want to get married or have any children. I want to always remain by myself."

FACTS: CHILDREN AND AIDS

As well as the possibility of being orphaned due to AIDS, children in many developing countries face a high possibility of contracting it themselves.

• In 2004, there were an estimated 15 million AIDS orphans worldwide; that number is expected to increase to 44 million by 2010.

• The AIDS epidemic has so far left behind 13.2 million orphans in sub-Saharan Africa, children fifteen years old or younger who have lost one or both parents to the disease.

• In some African countries, about 25 percent of all pregnant women are infected with HIV. Their babies may acquire HIV during pregnancy, labor, or delivery or through breast-feeding.

• Without preventive drugs, up to one-third of the babies of HIV-positive women will also become infected; most of these children will die by the age of eight.

• In developing countries, many HIV-infected children die from common childhood illnesses before their HIV is diagnosed.

• Children with HIV who are well fed get fewer infections and progress more slowly from HIV to AIDS.

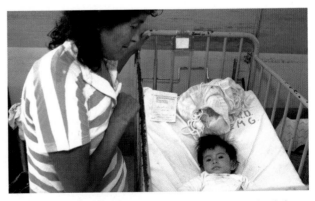

HIV can be transmitted from an HIV-positive mother to her baby before it is born and also through breast-feeding. It is possible, however, that the child will not catch the virus.

CHAPTER FIVE: Looking to the Future

It is impossible for children to prepare mentally and emotionally for life after a parent dies. The care and support that they need should not be underestimated. Thankfully, there are many organizations working in communities that are plagued by AIDS. These organizations offer help in the form of social workers and support groups to help AIDS orphans get through the hard times.

MARY SAYS ...

"I would like to be famous one day. I want to do two things, I want to be a mechanical engineer, and I would also like to be a pop singer.

If I was the president of South Africa, I would implement a law that all rapists be castrated. I would also make judgements on abusive parents much more severe. I would like to see them sent to a very dark prison with maximum security. I would also put all old people into proper nursing homes. I would also sponsor Topsy with lots of money each month.

One day, I would like to travel to Italy. I am interested in Italy, even though I don't really know much about it.

I would like to be like Elizabeth Moshe, Topsy's social worker, when I grow up. She is good-hearted and treats people well."

Organizations like the Topsy Foundation help young people like Mary by providing counseling and career-oriented training programs.

HAMBA KAHLE (GOODBYE)

Oh!! Mama wami *(Oh my mother)*

Indlu seyiwile *(My home has fallen)*

Akekho osoyose ayivuse *(No one to restore it)*

Lunjani usizi nokudangala *(How deep is the hurt and the disappointment)*

Kulawo mabele owawancelayo *(To the breasts that have fed)*

Nakulezo zandla ezakugonayo *(And to the hands that have comforted)*

Nakuleso sisu esakuthalayo *(And to the womb that has carried)*

Eminyakeni eminingi eyadlula *(Many years that have passed by)*

Ukuba namuhla uwuthwele ngesifuba *(But today your chest carries the heaviness of the soil)*

Ulala emvuleni ngabekunjani kulelo na? *(I wonder what it is like to be in the rain)*

Kepha indlela yethu sonke *(But we all are going that way)*

Lala sthandwa lala uphumule *(Rest my beloved, rest and be comforted)*

Written by Mary, 2004

HEALTH-CARE FACILITIES

In many parts of Africa, up to 80 percent of hospitals and clinics have too few doctors and nurses to deal with the enormous number of patients brought there by AIDS. As a result, many sub-Saharan governments have encouraged home-based care of patients.

Aid organizations give full training in caring for the sick and dying to the carergivers, many of whom are volunteers. Caregivers range from community health workers to family members, neighbors, and sometimes children who have had to drop out of school to help nurse a sick parent or relative. There is some concern that the quality of care available in these programs varies from one to another.

Aid organizations arrange for medical professionals and volunteers to visit AIDS patients in their homes.

DISTURBING PREDICTIONS

Experts predict that the AIDS pandemic will continue to escalate. They estimate that the number of AIDS orphans in sub-Saharan Africa will top 18 million by 2010.

The United Nations has warned that the pandemic could create a tidal wave of death affecting children around the world. By 2010, the average lifespan in Zambia will have dropped from sixty-six to thirty-three years, in Zimbabwe from seventy to forty, in Kenya from sixty-eight to forty, and in Uganda from fifty-nine to thirty-one years. The high number of people dying from AIDS at a relatively young age is the main cause of this decrease.

Southern Asia has one of the fastest growing HIV/AIDS epidemics in the world. Young people are especially at risk; there are already 1.2 million people below the age of twenty-five living with HIV/AIDS. Predictions are that the incidence of HIV/AIDS in the region could quickly grow to proportions seen in sub-Saharan Africa unless preventative measures are taken.

South Africa's president, Thabo Mbeki, has been criticized for questioning the connection between HIV and AIDS.

THE GOVERNMENT'S ATTITUDE

Over the last two decades, many people have criticized the South African government for not publicly acknowledging the extent of the threat that the AIDS pandemic poses to the country's people and its economy. President Thabo Mbeki's views on the causes and treatment of AIDS have also been widely attacked. Since 2000, Mbeki has funded a small group of scientists who claim that HIV does not cause AIDS. Mbeki has even gone so far as to admit he also does not believe there is a connection between HIV and AIDS despite overwhelming evidence to the contrary. Around the world, critics have accused

People living in poor communities in developing countries are the most vulnerable to catching HIV.

Many HIV/AIDS awareness campaigns are under way in countries like South Africa.

Mbeki's government of failing completely to respond adequately to the epidemic.

A MORE POSITIVE OUTLOOK

In the face of some dire estimates of the impact AIDS will have on the world in the next ten, twenty, or fifty years, it is encouraging to note that both global awareness and a drive to combat the disease are growing. Clearly, the international community and the governments of developing countries themselves are all making a concerted effort to tackle social taboos, gender issues, ignorance about practicing safe sex, and the lack of understanding and education about HIV and AIDS. These issues and many other factors of life in developing countries directly contribute to the rapid spread of the virus.

Many projects are underway to inform and educate people. A greater awareness of the illness; its effects on infected people, their family, and their community; and of how the

disease spreads, coupled with the energy of volunteers, medical professionals, and government representatives may help prevent the virus spreading to even greater numbers.

INTERNATIONAL ASSISTANCE

New strategies to combat the global HIV/AIDS pandemic emerge every day. Ultimately, however, what developing countries really need is financial assistance from affluent nations such as the United States and Japan and countries in Europe. In 2003, President George W. Bush pledged 15 billion U.S. dollars over five years to help combat AIDS in Vietnam and fourteen countries in Africa and the Caribbean. More money for health care, drugs, and education will be needed.

One fact is clear: the global AIDS problem is not going to simply go away. Countries like South Africa desperately need a continued international commitment.

About thirty-five thousand people from social serivce orgnizations work in South Africa. All are trying to tackle the further spread of HIV.

CHAPTER SIX: Those Who Help

AIDS has ravaged many parts of the world, but the hardest-hit area is undeniably Africa. Sub-Saharan Africa loses more than half a million of its people every year to the killer disease. In South Africa, the government has set up several organizations that work alongside many international aid agencies to address the growing problem. While there are a variety of opinions about how AIDS and HIV can be best fought, all agree that billions of dollars in financial aid are needed.

The twenty-first century has seen a rapid increase in the number of events to raise awareness of the global AIDS pandemic. The first South African National AIDS conference was held in 2002.

major steps in combating the AIDS pandemic. The United Nations and world governments can actually be held accountable for not meeting these targets. Already, progress has been made since this global initiative, with many countries pooling resources and experience to bring about change.

The Joint United Nations Programme on HIV/AIDS (UNAIDS) leads the international fight against the AIDS pandemic. Its goal is to stop the spread of HIV and to care and support people around the world suffering from the virus. UNAIDS was one of the main sponsors of the first South African National AIDS conference in 2002.

INTERNATIONAL ASSISTANCE

While certain parts of the world are more affected by the spread of AIDS than others, the disease is a global problem and a global responsibility. In 2001, the world's governments adopted the Declaration of Commitment on HIV/AIDS. This document established, for the first time, yearly targets for taking

MEDICAL ADVANCES

In many countries, scientists are conducting advanced medical research to attempt to stem the spread of AIDS. The Medical Research Council of South Africa (MRC) has many programs that focus on the public-health issues that cause the spread of HIV.

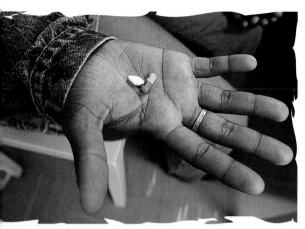

Medical breakthroughs have prolonged the lives of those with HIV, most notably, antiretroviral drugs.

In 2003, the South African government approved a Comprehensive National Plan on HIV and AIDS Care, Management, and Treatment. Under this plan, more than 1.4 million HIV-positive South Africans will receive antiretroviral treatment by 2008. Another medical organization helping victims is the African Medical and Research Foundation (AMREF), which runs community-based health care that is both lifesaving and affordable.

NONPROFIT AID ORGANIZATIONS

A nonprofit aid organization is an independent charity set up to help people in need. Any money these organizations raise or make is plowed back into their service programs. They play a major role in providing relief to victims of civil and military conflicts and natural disasters. Many of these organizations use volunteers who often produce faster and more effective results than many government programs.

This red ribbon is worn as a pin to symbolize a commitment to fighting the AIDS crisis.

CHARITIES IN ACTION

Many nonprofit aid organizations have been set up in South Africa to tackle AIDS. Here are just two examples:

• The Topsy Foundation works with rural communities in the Mpumalanga Province of South Africa, a region with a particularly high number of HIV-positive adults and children. It operates through three different programs: home-based medical care and social work for patients and their families; care at their own hospice facilities; and training programs that work to alleviate poverty.

• The charity SOS Children runs a social center in Mamelodi, South Africa. One of SOS Children's goals is to help and educate adults who want to take care of orphaned children. An outreach program cares for thirty-nine hundred orphans and offers employment to local youths.

To date, AIDS has made orphans of more than 5 million children. Researchers predict that by 2010, that figure will rise to 25 million.

HUMAN RIGHTS AND AIDS

When the AIDS crisis first began in South Africa, few people were aware of the human-rights issues this killer disease brought with it. South Africans with AIDS found themselves being discriminated against both professionally and socially. To tackle this problem, South African judge Edwin Cameron drafted the Charter of Rights on AIDS and HIV in 1992 to protect the rights of those infected with the virus. A wide range of local and international organizations and individuals, including political and religious leaders and artists, endorsed the charter. Since its launch, other countries, including Botswana and Namibia, have used the charter to draw up similar legal documents of their own.

In 1996, the Project Committee on HIV/AIDS was set up in South Africa. The committee produced reports that resulted in many major changes in the laws that affected the lives of people living with HIV and AIDS. One of these laws prohibited pre-employment testing for HIV, which meant that South African employers could no longer discriminate against prospective employees because they were HIV positive.

Many celebrities and political leaders have joined the fight against the spread of HIV/AIDS, including the former South African president, Nelson Mandela.

Bono, from the rock band U2, is a prominent spokesperson for the AIDS crisis.

CELEBRITY INVOLVEMENT

The Irish rock star Bono, from the band U2, is just one celebrity who has used his position to call on governments across the world to fight the AIDS epidemic in Africa. Bono has asked Western governments to use their financial resources and advanced technology to help reduce the conditions that have helped AIDS to flourish in Africa. His organization DATA (debt AIDS Trade Africa) calls on governments, political leaders, and the people of the West to help out. Another figure heavily involved is South Africa's former president, Nelson Mandela, whose son died of AIDS. Mandela helped to set up a volunteer campaign that attempts to persuade South Africans to volunteer their time to help the fight against AIDS. The campaign promotes safe sex, sharing information about HIV/AIDS with friends and family, and offering support to somebody with HIV/AIDS.

ECONOMIC HELP

The countries most affected by AIDS have little money to devote to programs for AIDS prevention, treatment, and care. Many of them are committed to repaying millions of dollars worth of loans to institutions such as the World Bank, the International Monetary Fund, and some Western governments.

Launched in 1998, the Jubilee 2000 Campaign called for canceling billions of dollars of debt owed by the world's poorest nations. The campaign has been partially successful, resulting in a certain amount of debt relief. Some developing countries, such as South Africa, can now devote more financial resources to fighting AIDS. In 2003, for example, the South African government pledged 1.7 billion U.S. dollars to fight HIV/AIDS over the next three years.

AN ONGOING APPEAL

While there is still a long way to go in fighting the AIDS pandemic, there is no denying that remarkable progress has already been made. In the last few years, the HIV/AIDS issue has become a major priority for governments worldwide. While many projects and initiatives have been implemented, still others are being discussed. The only way to combat an international crisis such as AIDS is by maintaining the global commitment to finding solutions.

HOW YOU CAN HELP?

1. GET POLITICALLY ACTIVE

Send an e-mail to political leaders, such as your senator or representative in Congress.

2. RAISE AWARENESS

Put a Stop Global AIDS Campaign poster in a prominent place. Wear an AIDS pin or ribbon every day. Tell people what it stands for and what they can do to help stop the crisis. Show an awareness-building video to friends and neighbors. Call a small meeting of members of your community to discuss ways you can help fight AIDS in your area and around the world.

3. ALERT THE MEDIA

Look for articles in your newspaper that offer a chance to send a short letter to the editor about the AIDS and debt crises. Call a talk radio program and suggest that it is time something was done to stop the global AIDS crisis.

4. VOLUNTEER

Find social service agencies working with people who have AIDS who need help with household tasks.

There are many things you can do to help children in parts of the world where AIDS is widespread.

Glossary

ABSTINENCE Refraining from something, such as having sex.

AIDS (ACQUIRED IMMUNE DEFICIENCY SYNDROME) A disease caused by HIV that causes a severe weakening of the immune system and makes a person vulnerable to all kinds of infections and illnesses.

ANTIBODIES Substances produced by the body that are released into the blood in response to bacteria, a virus, or any other foreign matter.

ANTIRETROVIRAL DRUGS Types of drugs used to treat HIV. While not a cure, they slow the spread of the virus in the body.

APARTHEID The system of South African laws (1948–1991) that separated and discriminated against people on the basis of race.

BEREAVED Suffering from the death of a loved one.

CIVIL WAR War between citizens of the same country.

COLOURED A South African term for a person of mixed race.

CONDOM A thin rubber sheath worn during sexual intercourse to prevent pregnancy and the infection of sexually transmitted diseases.

CONTAMINATED Infected or tainted by something dangerous, poisonous, or impure.

CONTROVERSY A public disagreement usually relating to an issue that many people have different opinions about.

DEMOCRACY A form of government in which citizens decide who is in power.

DEVELOPING COUNTRIES Poor countries that are seeking to become more advanced economically, politically, and socially.

DISCRIMINATION An unjust and unfair distinction between people, especially on the grounds of age, sex, race, or religion.

DIVERSITY Variety.

EPIDEMIC Infectious disease or illness that has spread widely in a community.

ETHNIC Way of distinguishing someone based on their place of origin or nationality.

FAMINE An extreme shortage of food across a wide area.

HIV (HUMAN IMMUNODEFICIENCY VIRUS) The virus that causes AIDS.

HIV POSITIVE A person who has tested positive in a blood test for HIV.

IMMIGRATION The movement of individuals into another country than where they were born.

IMMUNE SYSTEM System in the body that neutralizes potentially harmful bacteria and other alien substances that enter the body.

INAUGURATION Officially admitting someone, such as a president, to office.

INDIGENOUS Native to a particular place.

INEVITABILITY Event that is certain to happen.

INTRAVENOUS A drug that is administered into a person's veins.

MYTH An unfounded or false idea.

NDEBELE Native tribe of South Africa.

OPPRESSION Forcing someone to live in hardship.

ORPHAN A child whose parents are dead.

ORPHANAGES Institutions for the care of orphans.

PANDEMIC Infectious disease or illness that has spread widely over a whole country or large part of the world.

PREJUDICE Unjust opinion that is not based on reason or actual experience.

PROSTITUTE Someone who exchanges sex for money.

RAPIST Someone who physically forces another person to have sex with him or her.

REPRIMANDED Scolded or told off.

SEGREGATED Separated on the grounds of race, sex, or religion.

SENSATIONALIST Exaggerated language or descriptions often used by the media.

SIBLING A sister or brother.

STIGMA Mark of disgrace associated with a particular situation.

STRIKE To stop work or an activity to force a superior to change a situation.

SUB-SAHARAN The African regions south of the Sahara desert.

SYNDROME Group of symptoms that occur together and that characterize a particular illness.

TOWNSHIP South African community made up mostly of black people. Under apartheid, these were the official residential areas for black South Africans.

VIRUS An infectious substance that is able to multiply within the cells of a host organism, such as a human being.

VULNERABLE Open to attack or harm.

Further Information

AFRICARE
A private charitable organization that has been assisting Africa since 1970. Africare's HIV/AIDS Initiative works toward increased education on the disease, care for those who are already infected, and assistance for orphans. Their Web site includes topical articles about the latest news and statistics from Africa.
www.africare.org

AIDS.ORG
A Web site with a mission to help prevent HIV infection and to improve the lives of those affected by HIV and AIDS. The site also gives important information about how to get tested for the disease and how to prevent being infected.
www.aids.org

AVERT
An international HIV and AIDS charity that works to help with the problem of HIV/AIDS in countries where there is a particularly high or rapidly rising rate of infection.
www.avert.org

CRUSAID
Crusaid strives to make a difference to people living with and affected by HIV and AIDS. The organization also tries to reduce poverty and illness caused by the virus, as well as educating and supporting vaccine research.
www.crusaid.org.uk

PHYSICIANS FOR HUMAN RIGHTS
An organization of medical professionals that promotes health by protecting human rights. Using medical and scientific methods, it investigates and exposes violations of human rights worldwide and works to stop them. It educates health professionals and students about becoming active in supporting human rights in their work.
www.phrusa.org

THE TOPSY FOUNDATION
The Topsy Foundation works with rural communities in the Mpumalanga Province of South Africa, bringing about change through home-based and in-house care, community outreach support, and training and poverty alleviation programs.
www.topsy.org.za

WORLD HEALTH ORGANIZATION (WHO)
The World Health Organization is the United Nations' specialized health agency with the objective of gaining the best possible health for people all over the world. One of WHO's goals is to get everyone access to treatment and prevention methods to stop the spread of HIV and AIDS
www.who.int

Index